J. Archie.

# The Love of CATS

# The Love of CATS

## Christine Metcalf

OCTOPUS BOOKS

# Contents

First published 1973 by
Octopus Books Limited
59 Grosvenor Street, London W1

ISBN 0 7064 0227 8

© 1973 Octopus Books Limited

Distributed in USA by
Crescent Books
a division of Crown Publishers Inc
419 Park Avenue South
New York, N.Y. 10016

Distributed in Australia by
Rigby Limited
30 North Terrace, Kent Town
Adelaide, South Australia 5067

Produced by Mandarin Publishers Limited
14 Westlands Road, Quarry Bay, Hong Kong

Printed in Hong Kong

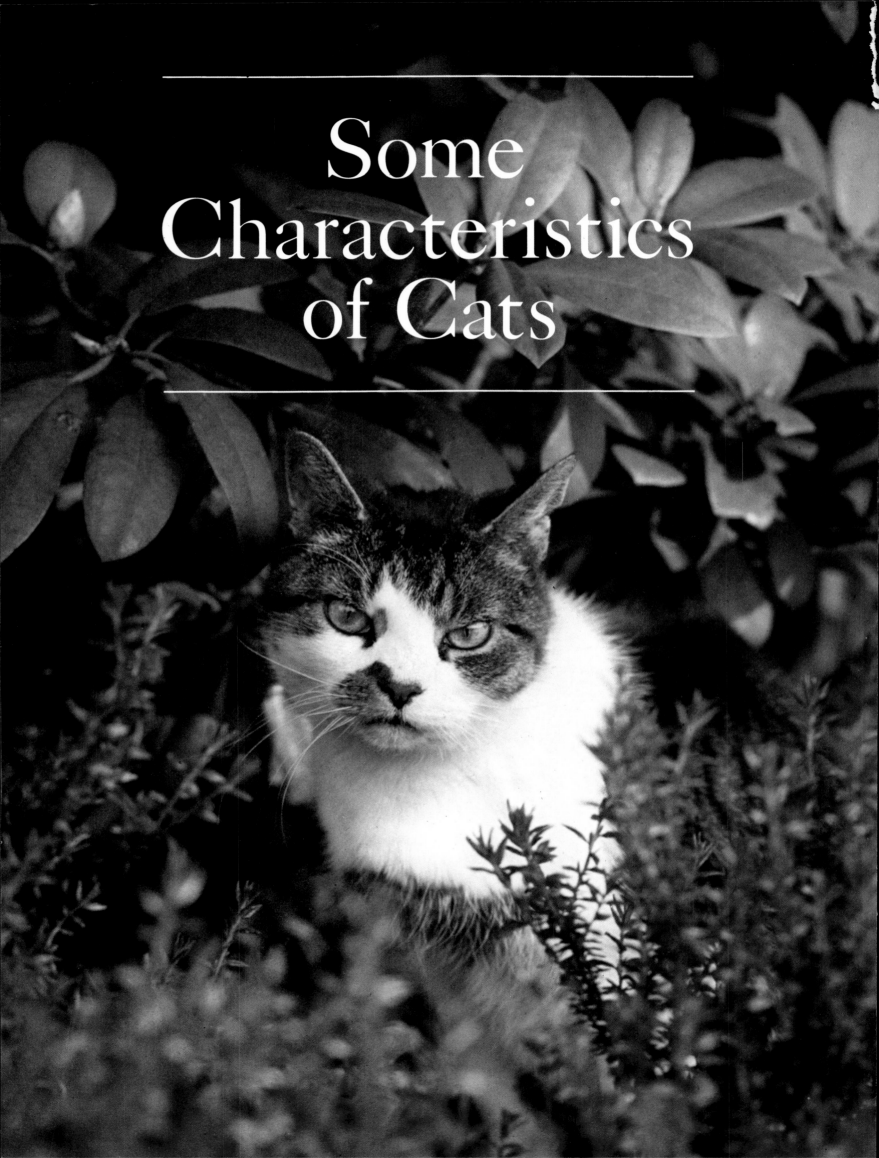

# Some Characteristics of Cats

'A cat is a lion in a jungle of small bushes.'
Thus wrote St George Mivart, an authority on cats in the nineteenth century, and watching a cat in the garden it is not difficult to relate it to its ancestors. Feeding upon other animals, which it must pursue with noiseless stealth and capture with sudden, controlled movements, the cat is built supremely for this life. It has padded feet which make no sound, and muscles of enormous power and bulk in proportion to its size which are attached to bones adjusted to each other at such angles as to form the most complete system of springs and levers for propelling the body known to the whole cat group. The claws are sharper and more curved into strong hooks than in any other mammal, and by action of special muscles are withdrawn under sheath-like pads, where they may escape injury and wear when not in use. No teeth are better fitted for their work, the great canines for tearing, and the scissor-like pre-molars for shearing off lumps of flesh small enough to swallow. In the eye, the fibres of the iris, opening to the widest extreme, expand the pupil to full circle admitting the darkness of night and by rapid and spontaneous contraction shut off all excess of blinding light at midday and permit minute exactness of vision under either extreme. There you have the cat, a piece of precision mechanism from lions down to domestic cats. All are able to move delicately on their toes, not on the soles of their feet, able to trot or, when speed is required, to speed along in great bounding leaps, each movement silently controlled by the great efficient muscles [*see next page*].
A cat's hearing is extremely acute, with the exception of white cats with blue eyes. Cats can detect sound far beyond the range of human hearing, and it has been suggested that a cat's hearing is more acute even than that of a dog. Each ear contains twenty-seven muscles, these enable the part of the ear we can see, the pinna, to be turned in several directions in order to collect sound waves. Siamese cats have enormous ears and breeders even encourage this feature as can be seen with this beautiful Tabby Point [*right*].
Most cats enjoy music and it is not unusual to see a cat stepping on the piano keys. They will often sit and listen to music as attentively as you do and have decided likes and dislikes.

[7]

Through the centuries the cat has been valued for its prowess in hunting. Even as long ago as 1,000 BC the cat was used in Japan and China to protect the silkworm cocoons from ravage by rats. In the ninth century in South Wales a prince called Hywel Dda, passed a law against killing a cat or its kittens because of their value in protecting the stores of grain. Today cats still perform a valuable service to the community by keeping down the rodent population. The wild instinct is deep-rooted in the cat and rodents are their natural food. A good cat will always eat a portion of its kill. However, this does not mean that the cat should be left to hunt for its own food. Working cats need more than milk if they are to keep in good condition. Well-fed cats and kittens will still hunt for sport and they need the vitality and stamina to do the job.

[8]

A cat will behave aggressively to dogs when they pose a threat to its territory or to its security. There is no threat when they share the territory, or in other words when they belong to the same owner, and so no need for aggression. Cats and dogs are not natural enemies.

When cats and dogs live together it is usually the cat who is in charge. The dog seems to accept this without question and then they become firm friends. I had a cat who would never let the dog snooze in the evening until they had had a game; she would tap and prod him and torment him until he would go after her. Pandemonium would break out and they would chase each other all over the house, the cat hiding and leaping out to surprise the dog again and again. You could almost hear them laughing as they romped around. When they had exhausted their fun they would curl up together and the dog would have his face licked clean as a reward. There was deep affection between those two.

We tend to think of working cats as being mongrel cats

catching mice and rats for us and throughout history this has been their role. Modern society however has created another niche for the working cat. There is now a great demand for more aristocratic cats to pose for photographic studies and many lovely pedigree cats are 'naturals'. These three [*above*] are certainly worthy picture-postcard cats: a beautiful Chinchilla (notice that he is smaller than the other Long-hairs), a Black Long-hair and a Smoke Long-hair. Persian cats and Siamese cats tend to be the favourite breeds for publicity and advertising, although Long-hairs have better temperaments. Everyone is familiar with the cats who appear regularly on our television screens in advertisements. Perhaps keeping a cat for this purpose seems a way to easy money, as an experienced model cat can earn up to two hundred pounds a day. However, a great deal of time and care goes into preparing a cat for this kind of life, it must be brought up to become accustomed to the atmosphere of a studio, the hustle, the lights and the heat and the hundreds of strangers.

A kitten cowers in his basket [*left*] frightened by the sudden appearance of the photographer . . . will he stand his ground or will he disappear quick as a flash to a safe place? He will probably settle back, since temperamentally the Colourpoint is a well-balanced cat. Although its ancestors are Siamese it has not inherited the noisy, demanding attitude of its grandsires, nor is it so highly strung. Colourpoints are hardy, gentle and affectionate, and they make delightful pets. They are quite content to be picked up and handled so they are happy in a household where there are children, providing care is taken to see they are not held carelessly or exposed to rough play, but this rule applies to all cats. Like all Long-haired cats the Colourpoint must be kept well brushed to retain the full beauty of the soft Persian coat. These cats are becoming more and more popular because on the one hand they are charming, elegant, and beautiful to look at yet at the same time they are very robust and easy to care for. Most cats are in fact very good at looking after themselves. The myth that cats have nine lives is well known; though what is usually meant is nine 'chances', as each time a cat has a narrow escape from an accident he is said to have lost one of his nine lives. Cats certainly seem to have some miraculous escapes and they also treat life with the greatest respect. A cat is by nature extremely cautious. It will not rush into a situation without first examining its surroundings. Open the door to let it out and it will size things up before it leaves the safety of the house. At night, it will hesitate while its eyes adjust to the darkness. Its reaction to sudden movement or noise is so swift that it can usually escape threatening danger, just as if a cat falls it nearly always lands on its feet.

The life-span of the cat is, on average, fourteen to fifteen years. This likely lad [*left*], called Blackett, is a veteran of eighteen years and he carries his age bravely.

The grin of the Cheshire cat may have been particularly large, but many cats enjoy a good joke and can grin almost as well as he [*top right*]. Cats have a sense of humour without a doubt and often have this expression as though laughing. They do not enjoy a joke against themselves however, nor do they like to be laughed at. They hate to be teased and they very rarely learn to do tricks just to amuse but if you are having fun they like to join in,

and they will certainly grin broadly at a joke against *you*.

A cat's face can be very expressive, it can show many moods: annoyance, fear, pleasure and pain. A cat with lots of personality may show its every reaction and thought on its face and you will learn to read it as you do human expressions. The eyes change colour, the pupils widen. The ears too, like the tail, can demonstrate various moods by the way they are held. It is fascinating to study the language of cats; every cat has its own character and as an individual it develops its own means of communication. All cats are vocal and all develop a language by means of gestures and expressions. Of course, some of the more basic gestures are common to all cats but there are so many that are special to the cat's own personality. A tail carried over the back but with the tip turned over, is an indication that this little ginger cat [*right*] is feeling pretty pleased with life and would even be quite aggressive towards another cat.

In literature cats are mostly praised for their intelligence, beauty and affection. Many writers had a favourite cat: Victor Hugo, Dr Johnson, and Charles Dickens, to mention a few. There is, however, the occasional writer who attacks the character of the cat. Georges Louis Leclerc Buffon, in the eighteenth century, wrote: 'The cat is an unfaithful domestic and kept only from necessity in order to suppress a less domestic and more unpleasant animal, and although these animals are pretty creatures, especially when they are young, they have a treacherous and perverse disposition which increases with age, and is only disguised by training. They are inveterate thieves; and when they are well brought up they become as cunning and flattering as human rascals.'

There are many millions of cat owners throughout the world who will feel indignant at such an opinion but the cat is not an animal to produce indifference, people either like them a great deal or they leave them well alone.

Kittens are by nature playful and full of mischief. They like nothing better than to leap around from one high place to another. It can leave you quite breathless just to watch them speeding across a garden and up into a tree in a matter of seconds. They are perfectly capable of amusing themselves and kittens who live together never seem to stop playing one game after another, many of them recognizable as 'hide and seek', 'I'm the king of the castle' and hunting games. This is where one kitten alone in a household can miss so much, as can you, and the responsibility of amusing him falls heavily on you. All kittens like to be entertained, however, and enjoy any toys they can roll about with or pounce upon, such as cotton reels, ping-pong balls, rolled-up paper, pipe cleaners and bits of string. Care must be taken to see that nothing they play with can be harmful in any way, or is small enough to be swallowed, for as with all babies, everything goes into the mouth.

These Blue Burmese are having a great time together but they could have a problem coming down the tree again, whereas the marmalade Tabby [*left*] looks as if he would like someone to come and play with him.

A magnificent set of whiskers and a smart new collar makes their proud owner [*left*] appear most dignified. The cat sheds its coat in spring and autumn and, of course, it is regrown. Whiskers are not shed with the rest of the coat, and are longer and grow in tufts. They feel coarse and wiry to the touch and are found on the tips of the ears, the eyebrows and on the mask of the face. The bulbs of the hairs are rich in nerve and blood supplies and their special function is to protect the eyes and act as very sensitive organs of touch.

It is a widely held belief that domestic cats use their whiskers to measure a gap before going through but few of the unfortunate overfed cats have whiskers to match their size. However, in a poor light this extra sense of touch can be a valuable asset, since the other widely held belief is that cats can see in the dark. This is, of course, a fallacy. They cannot see in complete darkness but they can see better than most mammals in a dim light. In its wild state a cat is nocturnal and does most of its hunting by moonlight; many pet cats still sleep by day and hunt by night. Many nocturnal animals can increase the amount of light passing through the retina because they have a reflecting layer in the choroid behind the retina, this is known as the tapetum. It is the tapetum which causes cats' eyes to shine at night when a bright light is directed at them.

The iris in cats' eyes is very contractile and is equipped with a dilating muscle which can respond suddenly to light changes. In a dim light, the pupil is widely exposed allowing the maximum light to pass through to the retina. In bright light, the opening contracts until all that is left of the pupil is a vertical slit.

A cat makes an ideal companion for anyone, but particularly for a lonely person. One cannot generalize, of course, but most cats will show much affection and in many different ways. Although the cat is independent it still has a need to be loved and will weave in and out of your legs or jump onto your lap when you sit down, or just sit close at hand purring loudly. When you go out it will often accompany you for a part of the way but it will not leave familiar ground, and on your return it will almost certainly be waiting close by ready to greet you as this Tortoiseshell and White is doing. When the cat is in the mood it likes to be fussed. You will soon be made aware of what pleases your cat. It may like to have its neck rubbed or to be stroked, each cat has its own preferences. Siamese cats are particularly affectionate and demanding, though often to only one person and they are really more like dogs in this respect.

Another unusual friendship [*below*] . . . this charming Persian and the jackdaw are old acquaintances and are fed together regularly.

Young cats spend a deal of time stalking birds and it is a long time before they discover the odds are against them. Kittens go quite wild with excitement chasing the birds in the garden but they do not often meet with success. As the cat matures it realizes the birds have the advantage of flight and it gives up trying, contenting itself with fledglings or the very old. Fewer birds than you would suspect are destroyed by cats but there would be even less if the cat was kept in at night. Cats like to hunt and they are most likely to attack at dawn when the birds are feeding and they are more vulnerable. Spring can be an anxious time for the bird lover who also loves cats, since so many birds build their nests in easily accessible places, possibly because increasingly large areas of woodland and hedge are being destroyed. Cats often know all about the nests and just wait for the day when the fledglings fly.

'Once upon a time there was a cat, a rabbit and a pekinese dog' [*right*] – these three look like a picture for a nursery tale. The cat will happily make friends with other animals providing a bit of caution is exercised at the introduction. A new kitten being brought into a household where there is already a dog in residence, or even another cat, must never be left alone with the older pets until it is clear they are friendly. The newcomer must not be fussed over too much in front of the old inhabitants who will be very quick to be jealous.

Cats are great poseurs, they have instinctive poise and dignity as well as playfulness, and that is why so many photographs of cats look posed: they are not at all, the co-operative cat will usually immediately position itself as well or better than a model as soon as it realizes it is the centre of attention. They also seem to know which colours in the garden and in the house will flatter their own coloration. They have an instinctive feeling for composition and once again the success of many photographs taken of cats in gardens is due less to the creative ability of the photographer than to the fact that he has had his camera handy at the right moment. The jet black coat of this cat contrasts magnificently with the rich salmon pink of the rhododendrons.

Cats are in fact, colour blind. They live in a black and white world where all colours are seen as shades of grey. It is all the more inexplicable how cats do have the knack of finding colours that suit them or show off their beauty but there are many cases to prove the point. It is one of the mysteries of the cat which remain unsolved.

# Kittens

A Chocolate Point Siamese Queen and her kittens aged four days [below]. When they are born Siamese kittens are pure white. The points will begin to darken after about one week, by the time they are a month old they will be recognizable as Siamese, and at about six weeks the points will have darkened sufficiently to establish the variety. Like all kittens Siamese are born blind but they begin to open their eyes after about three days which is earlier than other breeds.

There are usually about five kittens in a litter, although it has been known for there to be seven or eight. A litter of five is a good number for the mother to manage. When they are born they are about the size of mice, after a month they will begin to climb out of their box [below right].

Adorable, appealing, pretty, humorous, affectionate and irresistible – kittens are all these things. Passing a pet shop window with a litter of kittens on display can be a great trial for a mother with small children but she must pause for thought before giving in to the pleas to take one home. The kitten is a baby, and like a baby it will need care and attention. It will need warmth, frequent and regular meals and it will need loving; though not the fierce loving sometimes administered by some heavy-handed children, so they must be taught to handle the kitten tenderly. Caring for kittens does not require anything more than common sense. When it first

arrives leave it quietly to settle down. It will be feeling strange and frightened, and it will be missing its mother and its brothers and sisters. These Abyssinian kittens [right] will not appear in a pet shop. To obtain a pedigree cat you will have to go direct to the breeder.

Kittens should never be chastised for committing a misdemeanour. They will, without doubt, do something at some time to make you angry, they are notoriously mischievous and they certainly have no respect for property, but a kitten that receives harsh punishment will become less affectionate. If you strike a kitten you may hurt it more than you intended, since it has such tiny bones, and it will as a result feel insecure and maybe become nervous. You cannot make your cat do things, it must be encouraged or discouraged to do them. This is the form training should take and it should begin as soon as your kitten arrives. House training presents little difficulty as the cat is naturally clean, and so long as the means to be clean are provided, a sanitary tray at first and later, access to the garden, there should be no problem. If there is an occasional accident, possibly due to changes in diet, you should never rub the kitten's nose in it, but show him his tray to remind him that this is the proper place for this function.

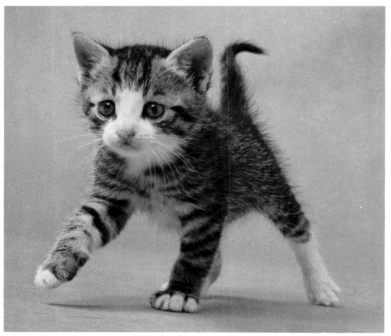

'Curiosity killed the cat' says the proverb. This may be so unless proper care is taken to protect the kitten from the hazards of our modern society. The kitchen is full of hidden dangers and an inquisitive kitten can come to grief if it is not kept away from the spin drier, washing machine, and dish washer. Gas cookers, electric stoves and hot saucepans can cause terrible burns and scalds if the kitten leaps up to see where the moving steam is coming from. Movement of any kind always attracts a cat so an open fire is also a source of danger, and it is wise to keep all fires guarded until your kitten has learnt about fire.

Cars are another danger to animals and an excited or frightened kitten is liable to dash into the road. If you live close to a busy road it is advisable to let it out only for short spells, keeping an eye on it all the time, or even to take it out on a lead.

Many kittens can be trained to the lead if you start early. Another thing to watch is backing your own car out of the garage as so often your animals will have followed you out of the house [*left*].

Usually you hear of people acquiring a kitten but I think the expression should be 'gaining a kitten'. You can go through the usual procedure of choosing your kitten, and take one home that is bright, healthy and has all the features you are looking for and once home you will begin to gain interest on your tiny investment; but, although you have chosen the kitten, it still has to choose to stay with you. The cat is very discerning and if it feels anything at variance with its own requirements, perhaps children that play too roughly, it will be away to make its own arrangements. Many people find themselves caring for cats that have just arrived out of the blue and have decided to make their home with them. A well grown, healthy kitten with shining coat, good claws and plenty of self confidence [*above*].

To keep your kitten healthy you must make certain it has the right minerals. Milk is an important source of calcium which is vital for young creatures, but some kittens refuse cow's milk. If your kitten refuses, calcium must be given by other means. Many manufactured foods are vitamin enriched. Liver will provide vitamin A which is important to growth, reproduction, resistance to infection, but it should not be given as more than one tenth of the cat's diet as it is addictive. Water, meat, offal and fish, vitamins, minerals and cereals are all necessary to a cat's diet.

# Genetics

The process of heredity is dependent on the genetic make up of the parents and the ultramicroscopic units of inherited material which are passed on via the genes to their offspring. Genes account for eye colouring, coat colouring, physical characteristics and sex determination.

Rex is the name given to gene mutations which cause the guard hairs in the coat to be absent. The undercoat, which is all we see on the Rex cat, is curly. The first Rex cats made an unexpected appearance on a farm in Cornwall, this was a natural mutation. From this cat a new breed evolved, the Cornish Rex. A few years later in Devon, another Rex kitten appeared, this time in a litter of foreign type kittens. The gene for the Devon Rex was quite a separate mutation. Whereas the Cornish Rex is soft and warm to the touch, and has a rather woolly coat, the Devon Rex has a closer coat which feels crisp and short. At first the coat of the Devon Rex was sparse and not particularly attractive but patient breeders have eliminated this feature and now the cat is adequately covered. Right is a Red Tabby Cornish Rex cat.

The Rex coat can be transferred to any colour or type of cat so although there are two standard Rex cats, Devon and Cornish Rex, any other breed can be produced with the typical wavy coat with an absence of normal guard hairs. The standard for Russian Blue cats [*left*] set out by the American Cat Fanciers Association states that it is a dainty cat distinct from all other breeds with its soft, lustrous, bright blue double coat, to handle it feels like running a silk scarf through your hands. If the Rex coat factor is introduced into the breeding plan of a Russian Blue it at once removes one of its typical features, the double coat. At the same time experimental breeding in the past has produced some very beautiful varieties so it is not to be discouraged but it must be handled with care and only by very experienced breeders.

A normal cat has five toes on each of its front feet and four toes on each hind foot as shown below on these Burmese kittens, but it is not uncommon for it to have extra toes. This condition is known as polydactylism. It is known to be inherited but details of the inheritance are unknown. Geneticists believe that it is a characteristic determined by a dominant gene which may express itself in various way. Sometimes the irregularity is passed directly to all the kittens, sometimes to only half. On occasion all the kittens in a litter from a polydactyl parent will be normal but they in turn can transmit extra toes to subsequent generations.

Matings between black and tabby cats strongly support the idea that the gene for tabby markings is dominant over black. Tabby cats can be striped or blotched. In the striped tabby, the sides of the body are marked from shoulder to tail with narrow, vertical stripes, whereas the blotched tabby has longitudinal stripes forming a horseshoe or circular pattern. When a mating takes place between a striped and a blotched tabby, the striped pattern is dominant. The Silver Tabby mother with her young offspring [above left] is a blotched tabby as the stripes can be seen running horizontally on her chest and neck.

The dominant gene for tabby marking will invade any colour coat but on none can the pattern be seen more clearly than on the Short-haired Silver Tabby [left]. The intense black of the marking shows up extremely well against the ground colour of pure silver. The standard for the tabby pattern expects that on the shoulder there should be oval markings, distinct and regular in outline so that if the coat could be removed and viewed from the top, the head markings together with those on the shoulder, would create the impression of a butterfly.

When a number of Tabbies are together the variations in pattern are obvious but on each individual cat it will be seen that the two sides correspond fairly evenly so that the cat appears well balanced.

An interesting combination is this Abyssinian crossed with a Silver Tabby [above]. If the breeder wished to show it, the 'Any Other Variety' section is the only one available. Silver Tabbies are British Short-hairs with a silver background colour and tabby markings in black. Abyssinians are the 'little lion' cats with foreign type bodies and ticked coats in either brown or red. A new variety of cats is produced when a breeder transfers the features of one breed to those of another. Even if that is successful it takes several generations of breeding back so that the result is predictable and kittens breed true.

The features of two breeds of cat in one can be clearly seen here. The head has the typical Abyssinian appearance, wedge shaped with oriental eyes, the coat obviously ticked but the colouring is inherited from the Silver Tabby, and so too, are the tabby markings.

These two kittens [*left*], one tortoiseshell and white and the other orange, show clearly the genetic difference of coloration between male and female. Orange is the geneticists' term for red, yellow and marmalade coat colour. Tortoiseshell is peculiar in that the colour is made up in distinct patches. The reason is that small parts of the body show the effect of the orange influence which is only completely dominant in the male, the rest of the coat in a female is made up with the other normal colours. An understanding of cat genetics is a necessary, if complex, part

of cat breeding. There is a need to know something about the basic units of inheritance and many good books have been published which explain the subject very thoroughly.

The Manx cat [*above*] is an animal with a genetic difference. It does not conform to the basic pattern of cats, since it has no tail, or if it does have one it is never more than half a tail. Since there has to be an explanation for all things, an assortment of legends exists to account for the Manx cat's loss. It has been said that Irish warriors removed the tails to decorate their shields and helmets. To

prevent this happening the anxious mother cats bit off the tails of their kittens at birth. Noah is supposed to have slammed the door of the Ark on the tail of the last cat to enter. Some tailless cats from Spain are supposed to have swum ashore after the Armada, and Manx cats are said to be descended from these. These stories merely convey that they are of unknown origin. There is no real evidence that they originated on the Isle of Man, although a cattery has been established on the island, and the Manx is also featured on the reverse side of a coin in their currency.

solid legs. There was nothing foreign in its appearance at all. The owner could not account for this as there was no Siamese in the neighbourhood that could have sired the kitten. One possible solution lies in the white mother. Since white is dominant there may have been some Siamese in her family line but the colouring was masked by the white gene, making a re-appearance a generation or so later. This is what has happened here [*left*]; the Havanna Brown was bred from Black Long-hairs and Siamese; and this cat has had a 'throw-back' kitten – a pure Siamese.

Genetically speaking, white is dominant over all other colours. A white cat will pass on the white colouring to about half its kittens. This can clearly be seen from the hundreds of neighbourhood cats who carry large patches signifying their mixed ancestry. The vast majority of mongrel cats carry white areas in their coat [*below*], in combination with the other basic colours of black, red, tabby, blue and cream. Tortoiseshell-and-white, black-and-white and tabby-and-white are the obvious examples. Breeding for colour purity and texture of coat is an absorbing part of the business for all breeders but it is particularly so when cats with white as a part or the whole colour of their coat are involved.

It is interesting to note that in many other small animals the dominance of white over other coloured coats does not exist. If it did, of course, it would mean that all wild creatures would carry white patching and this would destroy their camouflage.

A very unusual kitten once appeared in a litter of farmyard kittens. The sire was a black mongrel cat and the mother was white. The kitten had beautiful Siamese colouring, pale cream shading to a deeper fawn, the mask, ears, feet and tail of a deep rich brown. The striking fact about this kitten was that the colouring had transferred to a Short-hair type, round head, cobby body on

This little marmalade cat [*right*] is a young tom. Colour is an inherited characteristic, as is eye colour, physical character and sex determination. Differences in development are due to the different genes. The gene whose influence is most exhibited is known as the dominant gene. Sometimes a gene is said to be sex-linked and when a gene alters it is known as a mutation. The mutant yellow gene of cats results from a mutation in the gene for extension of black pigment throughout the coat. It is carried in the sex chromosome which means it is sex-linked. The yellow mutation is incompletely dominant so that it is handed to male kittens as all-yellow or all-black, and to female cats as tortoiseshell. Occasionally a yellow female will appear in a litter and very rarely a tortoiseshell male but when this occurs the male is almost always sterile.

# Cats on the Roof-top

There are not so many stray kittens now, nor is it always easy to find a kitten when it is wanted. Mongrel kittens are not so plentiful now that more females are being spayed. This is a very good thing as it prevents unnecessary distress. Information about where to obtain a kitten can usually be got from the animal welfare societies, or there may be an advertisement in the local newspaper. There always seem to be postcards in the vets' waiting rooms asking for good homes for unwanted kittens. The cat population is represented mainly by mongrel cats throughout the world and in Britain there are an estimated twelve million. In the United States there are probably twice that number.

The cat has a wicked charm all its own. It is often a rogue and a thief. It has no respect for personal property and will steal the meat from your plate if you turn your eyes away. The cat's natural instinct leads it to forage for food and if it smells something good, the Sunday joint or fish for your supper, you only have yourself to blame if it disappears. Everything must be put out of temptation's way.

When you are training your kitten it is wise from the start to scold it when it jumps onto the table. A firm reminder when it repeats the action will make it clear that you do not approve, but this is no guarantee that it won't do this when your back is turned. There is only one way to prevent your cat from stealing and that is to keep food out of reach in a cupboard which the cat cannot open.

Cats are notoriously promiscuous. An unchecked female will go on producing kittens almost *ad infinitum*. Fortunately most pet cat owners are very responsible and they make sure that their tom cats are neutered and their female cats are spayed. It is much better for kittens to be neutered if they are to be kept purely as pets. For one thing, an unneutered tom will spray carpets and curtains and leave unpleasant smells, and it is almost impossible to keep a female inside once she is in season. Should she find a male, and this would not be difficult since hopeful males would hear her calling and would be waiting for her, the gestation period is sixty-five days. Almost immediately after kittening she will come into season again. Apart from the difficulty in finding good homes for vast numbers of kittens, it is very debilitating for the mother.

When the males in the neighbourhood hear the call of a female they will gather in groups to court her. You can hang out of your bedroom window throwing old boots or just bury your head under the blankets but you will never cut out the sound of the tom cats caterwauling on the rooftops serenading the lady. What is more, the noise is only the beginning. There follows the fight to find the strongest male, who will then be the first to serve the queen. The fighting is bloody and silent and while it is in progress the female is twisting and posing, waiting for the triumphant male. When battle is over the queen may be served rapidly in succession by all the males present. When the resulting litter is born there will probably be a collection of different coloured kittens because they could have been sired by several different males.

Cats have been known to strike up a friendship with all kinds of animals. One family I know own a cat, a dog and a guinea pig. The three animals are inseparable and when the family go away on holiday the boarding kennels take all of them together. There is another cat which sleeps in the hay bag of a horse belonging to a well-known brewery. Cats have even been known to make friends with pet mice. My own cat spends a lot of time in the run with the tortoises but I haven't yet discovered whether it is friendship or just plain curiosity, she spends a great deal of time patting and poking them.

Cats prefer living in a household with other animals, particularly do they like to share their home with another cat. If you go out to work and leave the house empty it really is a good idea to have two or three of them.

homeless animals, for many people allow their cats to breed freely hoping to find homes for the kittens when they are born. These mongrel cats, the result of free mating over many years, are more representative of the cat population than any of those described by the Cat Fanciers Associations throughout the world. Most of them are short-haired in any of the recognized colours or variations of them. Most of them have tabby markings and, or, patches of white. Their bodies are usually cobby and solid.

Vast numbers of 'moggies' are kept as working cats all over the land, particularly on farms where they are invaluable to the farmer in keeping down the rodents who would otherwise devour cattle feed, seeds and stocks of grain. Most farmers employ the services of a family of cats in exchange for board and lodging.

There is usually a working cat to be found on board ship; this is a very old tradition. Many legends have arisen from the cats that have travelled widely in this way. Sailors have several superstitious fears concerned with cats on ships. A cat that attaches itself to a ship is certain to be well cared for, sailors are well known for their kindness to animals. The cat has complete freedom in port but when it is at sea it has to learn to cope with hazards quite unlike those of a land cat.

Some people have asked if their much loved pet cat can be exhibited at the show even though it has no pedigree, and there is the class for household pets in which the points are awarded for condition.

Most shows have a section for pet cats. The section is divided into a number of classes which may include awards for the most luxurious coat, sleekest coat, largest eyes, most appealing and most unusual expression. There is an award for working cats and for numerous other characteristics. A small fee is payable for each class entered and the cat may be entered for any for which it is eligible. All kittens entered must be over two months old, if over three months old they must be inoculated at least three weeks prior to the show. Toms over nine months must be neutered.

Entries close about six weeks before the date of the show. Anyone interested in showing a cat should apply at least two months in advance for an entry form and show schedule.

Hundreds and thousands of cat lovers in the world today are perfectly satisfied and even prefer to have a pet cat without a long history of its inheritance as they are often very attractive [above] and have masses of character. What a blessing it is that non-pedigree cats are so well-loved or there would be a vast community of

body and character. They keep away from human contact as much as possible. There is a hospital in South London where there are dozens of these cats living in the service ducts beneath, scavenging for their food and multiplying rapidly. There are large feral cat populations in most areas of the world. The Colosseum in Rome is inhabited by vast numbers of feral cats increasing in numbers all the time. Florence, too, has a large number of them. Feral cats are large and aggressive, and any pet wandering into their territory is in danger of being attacked.

Stray cats should not be fed unless it is known for certain that they are strays. Should a stray turn up on your doorstep looking in need of a square meal you should feed it somewhere outside the house, as the life of a stray is hard and being a prey to disease of all kinds, it is certain to have parasites in its coat. It could be a serious threat to your own pet cat with whom it may come into contact, and if you decide to invite it to stay as a permanent resident it would be as well for a veterinary surgeon to see it before it enters the house.

Cats without a pedigree are no less adored than those with a long family tree. They make equally good, sometimes better pets, they are amusing, intelligent, affectionate and in every way they make delightful companions.

This kitten is lively and is ready for a romp just as soon as the invitation of that look is accepted. If the owner is too busy to play it is perfectly capable of finding something mischievous to do. My own kitten regularly has all the cacti out of their pots, and she seems quite undeterred by the prickles. If there is nothing else to do then a snooze curled up on a woollen pullover is the very least any cat can ask for.

Many cats become strays when their owners move house or go away on holiday and of course this is a deplorable way of treating a cat. It is more likely to happen when the male has not been neutered or the female spayed, although some cats are just born wild, they are strays at heart.

These strays [*below*] are known as feral cats; they have two aims, to feed themselves and to procreate. They are tough in

[44]

# Long and Short-haired Breeds

In ancient times the Indian Desert Cat was often tamed and kept as a domestic cat. Its colour, for complete camouflage, was a sandy yellow with round black spots and brown ear tufts. This Red-spotted cat could perhaps trace its ancestry to such a source for it has a wild look about it. Spotted cats are as old as time yet they are among the newest entrants at the shows. The reason for this is that in a pedigree cat the spots must be clear and distinct, and must contrast well with the background colour. Stripes and bars anywhere but on the face and head would be quite wrong for a pedigree cat. You can imagine the kind of difficulties this can present for a breeder.

'*Batchelor Buttons*', this Blue Spotted cat, might look barred or striped if he were relaxed. The rosette shaped or round spots show to better advantage when the cat is in motion. Blue spots may be seen on a silver or cream background, other spotteds are found in many of the combinations of colours found among the British Short-hairs. Body shape, too, conforms to the standard set out for British Short-hairs, or Domestic Short-hairs as they are called in the United States. To the inexperienced breeder the kittens may at first be a disappointment for they appear to have lines of solid colour down the spine. These often break up as the cat matures.

One of the loveliest cats imaginable is the Chinchilla. Its eyes are sea-green, dark rimmed as if wearing eye make-up, and its flowing white coat appears to sparkle with silver. It is no wonder this cat is in constant demand for modelling and for appearance on television.

The Chinchilla is a little smaller than most other Long-haired cats. The undercoat is pure white, the hairs of the top coat are tipped with black which gives it this tinsel effect. The coat is thick and soft, a great deal of grooming is needed to keep it in good condition. Like all long-haired varieties, the Chinchilla has a long frill around the neck, the tail should be short and bushy, the leather of the nose is brick red, the pads black or brown.

Chinchillas used to be divided into two classes, Silver Persians and Shaded Silver Persians. It became so difficult for the judges to decide to which class each belonged that the Shaded Silvers were abandoned in Great Britain. The American Cat Fanciers Association continues to recognize the darker variety, in which the undercoat is more grey than white. The Shaded Silver is also recognized in some countries of the British Commonwealth.

Some breeders have tried crossing the Chinchilla with the Blue Persian and they now produce the Blue Chinchilla. The coat of this lovely cat is ticked with blue rather than black which looks most distinctive. It is not yet, however, a recognized breed and can only be shown in the class for 'Any Other Variety'.

Chinchillas are not very prolific, nor is it easy to breed the purity of colour which is demanded, for this reason good show specimens are particularly sought after. They may be descendants of cats bred from a Long-Haired Silver Tabby crossed with a Tortoiseshell and White. The established variety in Britain has black ticking which gives a white cat, or, what at first appears to be a white cat, its sparkling appearance.

Identical with the Chinchilla, but with the ticking in red, is the Cameo [*above*]. There are four shades of Cameo cats, recognized in the United States but not in Britain. Their colour, a combination of cream and red, has been developed over a period of twenty years in America. In the Shell Cameo the colour of the undercoat should be the very palest cream, and the hair on the back, flank and head should be lightly tipped with red. The Shaded Cameo has shading that is considerably heavier, while the Smoke Cameo has the deepest colour of all. The fourth member of the group is the Tabby Cameo which has well defined beige or red tabby markings.

One of the most difficult of the tabbies to produce is the Red Tabby [*above*]. Ginger cats are sometimes mistakenly called 'Red' when the colour is really sandy yellow or marmalade. A true Red Tabby has markings of a deep mahogany red on a ground colour of rich red. White hairs or spots or a white tip to the tail are considered bad faults. The eyes should be hazel or orange, the marking must conform to the general pattern for all tabby cats.

The difficulty for breeders is in producing a marked distinction of colour

between the pattern and the ground since they are both shades of the same colour.

There are two basic Tabby patterns, one is striped the other blotched. Tabby cats have a base colour over which lines of a darker colour are superimposed forming a pattern of lines, spots or small patches. Cats with tabby markings are most similar to the wild cat, which also has this pattern on its coat.

This rather serious looking tabby [left] clearly demonstrates the 'M' on its forehead. This is a typical pattern

formation where the lines running down from the head turn towards the nose and the top of the eyes. It is said that the cat was once caressed by Mahommet and where his fingers touched there is now an imprint on the shoulders. Perhaps he also left his initial on the cat's forehead. The Cornish Rex cat [above] was a chance happening. It was on a farm in Cornwall in 1950 that this cat first made an appearance. A pair of farm cats produced a litter of kittens and among them was a kitten with a peculiar curly coat. It was unusual because all other cats have coats

with straight hair. The owner at once recognized that the kitten was unique and when it reached maturity it was mated back with the mother in an attempt to reproduce the strange appearance. Half of the resulting litter was born with this peculiar, short, silky coat. The hair on the body was much shorter than that of the normal short-haired cat, each individual hair was waved and no guard hairs were visible because they were shortened to just below the level of the top coat. Even the whiskers and eyebrows were crimped.

The Cream Long-haired cat [*above*] has a long flowing coat of delicate ivory. Ideally the colour should be true throughout the coat, with each hair unshaded from the root to the tip. Quite a few of these cats have a light tummy and a white tip to the tail, and bars sometimes appear on the legs all of which would lose points at a show. Breeders try to produce a cool colour as there is a tendency for the shade to become hot, more of a warm apricot than a cool cream. It is said these cats were the result of mating Blue males with Red females but breeders now avoid the Reds and keep the colour pale by mating the Creams with Blues. These cats have wonderful eyes: they are a beautiful deep copper in colour, and set against the pale fur, shine like jewels. The kittens are like all Persian kittens, just balls of fluff and look in particular like day old chicks!

Sometimes the Blue-Cream Persian is called the Blue Tortoiseshell. This name is more applicable to the Blue-Creams of the United States where the colours may be in solid patches [*top right*]. In Britain, and on the Continent, the colours must be softly intermingled giving the hazy appearance of watered silk. The colours must be pastel shades of blue and cream. As in all long-haired cats, the coat must be long and flowing.

The eyes should be deep orange or copper coloured. Like the Blue-Cream Short-haired cats these Long-hairs are not easily obtained because of the difficulties in breeding them. Blue-Cream kittens are enchanting in their curiosity and sense of fun, they are bold and intelligent. A grown cat is a charming companion, placid and delightful in every way.

Recognized only in the United States, the Peke-Faced Persian [*right*] gets its name because its features closely resemble those of the Pekinese dog. It has the same heavy jowls and large, prominent ears, which have an expression quite unlike that of other Persian cats. The forehead is high and bulges over the nose to create a sharp stop. The nose is very short, depressed and indented between the eyes. Like the dog in profile, the nose of the cat is so short that it is hidden by the full, round cheeks. There are wrinkled folds of skin cascading from under the eyes and each side of the nose. This extra skin often causes the tear ducts to become blocked so that the huge eyes are apt to water a great deal and spoil the cat's appearance when the fur on the cat's face becomes stained. In temperament and build this cat conforms to the standard set out for Persians. It was first developed from Red Tabby

and Solid Red Long-hairs and these are
the colours for which there are classes,
any signs of white are penalized. The eyes
should be brilliant copper or deep orange
in colour.

The Silver Tabby, whether it be Long- or
Short-haired, is of outstanding
appearance [*Following pages*]. The contrasts
of the black and silver are most striking.
During recent years there has been a new
interest in this breed, though at one time it
was in danger of dying out. They are now
seen in increasing numbers in Britain, on
the Continent and in the United States.
The Silver Tabby Short-haired cat is an
ideal choice for someone living on their
own, as it is extremely affectionate and
enjoys human company. It is not in any
way demanding, in fact it tends to be
very unassuming. The standard they
conform to is as for all British Short-hairs.

The eyes are green or hazel and well rounded, the body may vary in size according to colour. Those with very contrasting coats tend to be long and lean, those with a pale silver ground colour and softer coats are well-knit and stocky.

The Long-haired Silver Tabby [*right*] is one of the rarest cats in the cat world. The ground colour is pale, cool silver marked with dense black markings in the patterns described as for striped or blotched Short-hair tabbies. The long flowing coat tends to obscure the pattern and so owners aim to make the coat very smooth. The cat should be groomed both ways at once, downwards from shoulder to tail and upwards from the shoulders to the head.

The name tabby originates from the Eastern striped or water-marked silk known as 'attabi' which comes from Bagdad. The stripes and whorls on the cat's coat reminded a buyer of the pattern on the silk material and so the name was transferred to the animal.

Bi-coloured Long-haired cats may be found in combinations of red and white, black and white, cream and white, and blue and white. These are the recognized varieties and of these black and white are the most common and are often called Magpies. Since so many of the neighbourhood cats seem to wear these colours you may at first wonder what is so special about this breed. In fact, perfection for the show bench is not easy to achieve for the pattern demanded by the judges is very exacting. The two colours must be in equal quantities, with the colour solid on the tail but evenly broken on the body and face, there must be no tabby marking on the self-coloured portion. Ideally, the shoulders, neck, front legs, feet and chin must be white, the ears and mask should be self-coloured but there should be a white blaze up the face and over the top of the head, so that the face is divided equally in half. The standards set out for these colour pairings are the same both for Long-haired cats and their Short-haired counterparts. This kitten [*below right*] is very endearing, but it is not marked according to the strict show standards.

A cat that can truly trace its ancestry back to Thailand is the Korat [*following page*]. No need for legend or myth to describe its origin, for the Korats of the United States and other countries can trace a line directly back to stock exported from Thailand. A Korat Cat Fanciers Association was formed in 1965 to develop the breed and to protect its natural form during the course of its development. There are some breeds which move right away from the original aims of the breeders and Korat Cat Fanciers do not wish to see this happen. The Korat is medium in size and is well muscled. It has elegant legs with dainty oval paws. The tail is of medium length and may have kinks. The head is small with a heart-shaped face, particularly in the males, who have an indentation

between the ears, which accentuates this effect. The large, prominent eyes are bright green or amber, the ears are wide based and rounded at the tips. The particular characteristic of this cat lies in its colouring. The coat is a solid slate blue with each hair silver-tipped so the Korat appears bathed in moonlight. The leather of its nose and pads is dark lavender blue.

The lucky, or unlucky, black cat [*right*] is more rare than you would suspect, especially as a show cat. The standard requires the coat should be jet black with not a single white hair, and the eyes must be deep copper or orange. There must be no green in the eyes at all which is a point to watch since these cats do tend to develop a green rim which is quite unacceptable. In type the cat is the British or Domestic Short-hair, well knit and powerful. The overall appearance is one of general activity, states the standard, but like all cats they are expert in the art of relaxation.
An interesting aspect of black cats is that they are really tabbies with the black tabby pattern overlaid on a jet black background. We know this because the pattern can be clearly seen in young kittens before the coat darkens.
The beauty of the Long-haired Black cat [*left*] is undeniable and many people think they are the most beautiful of all the Long-hairs. However if you are thinking of showing, this is a very difficult breed to present successfully. Hairs of any other colour stand out quite clearly against the raven black coat and, it is a colour which very easily spoils so extra care is needed before the show. If a black cat walks frequently through wet grass its paws and legs can become rusty coloured, so a show cat sometimes leads a restricted life, particularly as the black hairs may also be bleached by the sun. All cats love to lie in the sun and a Long-haired Black is no exception but this can have a detrimental effect on its coat. Depth of colour does not develop until a kitten is six months old so that a breeder has a serious problem when he wants to be sure he is choosing the best kitten for the show as most of them are a rusty brown.

Tortoiseshell, but it has white patches added. In this variety of cat all the patches must be of solid colour and there should be no tabby markings on any part of the body. The white must be equally balanced with the other colours but as white is dominant there is always a tendency for it to be most in evidence. It is obvious from this that it is not so simple to breed a good specimen, especially with the added difficulty of the sex-linked yellow gene which is so unpredictable. *Right* is a magnificent specimen of an orange-eyed Long-haired White.

The physical appearance of the Colour-point [*below left*] must be cobby, with short, sturdy legs, and a round, broad head with the ears wide apart. The face and nose must be short, and the tail too should be short and full. In fact, the all-over impression must be of a soft roundness. The colouring is as for Siamese with the appropriate mask and points, that is cream with seal, magnolia with lilac, glacial white with blue and ivory with chocolate. The points must be of solid colour and any body shading must tone with the points.

Seal and Blue Colourpoints are the most popular colour combinations, but Chocolate and Lilac are close runners up. Below is a Blue Point. In 1970 there were some new arrivals to the show benches when Colourpoints made their appearance with Red and Tortoiseshell points and masks. These have been seen among the Himalayans in the United States for some time. The American Cat Fanciers Association know the Lilac as Frost Point.

The Blue Persian [*right*] is often regarded as the cat most likely to succeed in the show ring. A good specimen is almost perfect. Because of the quality of the coat it is a breed often used to improve the standard of other Long-haired varieties.

The body type is typical of the Long-hairs, big but not ungainly, with round and broad head, tiny, well-tufted ears showing a good width between them. The eyes should be large and round, brilliant orange or copper red in colour. The colour of the coat ranges from the palest lavender to deep sapphire. It is important for the show cats that the colour is uniform throughout. It can be light, medium or dark blue but there must be no patches of white hairs in the coat. The frill must be the same colour as the fur on the other parts of the body, a pale frill is considered a fault.

Portrait of a magnificent if fierce-looking cat [*above*]. The requirements for the Long-haired Tortoiseshell and White are as for all Persian cats. The coat must be long and flowing, extra long on the brush and frill. The body must be cobby and massive on short legs. The round and broad head should have small, tufted ears, set well apart, with a short, broad nose and full, round cheeks. The three basic colours, black, red and cream should be distinctly patched and interspersed with white. Eye colour for this variety is deep orange or copper. In America this breed is known as the Calico Cat. The American Cat Fanciers Association prefer that one side of the face be black and the other side red or cream, they like the white markings to be limited to certain areas so that the cat looks as if it has been dropped into a can of white paint.

Tortoiseshell colouring is transferred almost always to the female kittens only. Tortoiseshell and Tortoiseshell and White both have class numbers allocated to them by the Governing Council of the Cat Fancy in Britain and the American Cat Fanciers Association in the United States.

The Tortoiseshell and White has the same basic colouring as for the

# The Well-cared for Cat

Your new kitten will be eight to ten weeks old when you take it home. It must, of course, be completely weaned from its mother before it is removed. It is going to require five or six meals a day, spaced at intervals of between three and four hours. Like babies, kittens need to eat little and often. Three or four of the meals need only be a little milk with cereal or egg, but you should give a small quantity of raw beef or cooked meat at least twice a day. Vary the diet as much as possible, some minced raw liver, cooked and boned fish or cooked rabbit are ideal. Do remember to give your kitten fresh water to drink, milk alone is not sufficient liquid. The number of meals can be reduced to four when the kitten is about twelve weeks old, but the amount must be increased. Cut down to two meals when the kitten is six months old, one in the morning and one in the afternoon. Incidentally, if you are feeding several kittens it is much better to give them individual dishes. Cats are fastidious about their food. They have definite likes and dislikes, each one is different. They cannot be trained to do tricks for the reward of food like many other animals, nor can they be made to eat foods that are not to their taste. A high protein diet is their natural fare and most cats will turn from proteins of vegetable origin. They like meat, liver and fish. Care must be taken not to indulge your cat, however, wrong feeding and over-feeding lowers a cat's vitality. If it refuses food that you know to be suitable you must persevere. Many of the tinned cat foods are highly suitable and very convenient for the owner but some raw meat should be given regularly. Do not give lamb, chicken or rabbit raw, this should always be cooked and served straight from the refrigerator.

When a kitten is about six months old it sheds its milk teeth.
In its lifetime it has two sets of teeth. The second set are the
typical teeth of the carnivore; the two long sharp teeth in
front with which to catch and kill their prey, and the sharp
edged molars which can pare meat from the bone, but they
have no flat teeth with which to chew their food. Cats do not
usually suffer from tooth decay but they do sometimes get
prorrhoea, a disease caused when deposits of tartar build up

on the teeth, pushing the gums away and exposing the roots. When infection invades the socket, inflamation and loosening of the teeth is the result and this in turn causes digestive troubles. In its natural state a cat's teeth get plenty of use. Too much soft food can cause them to deteriorate. An occasional raw, meaty bone to chew upon, or some of the hard dry foods rather like biscuits now available, can do much to prevent trouble with teeth.

It has often been said that cats attach themselves to places, not to people. Personally I would not agree with this as my own cat moved house with my family six times and whilst the cat adjusted to its new surroundings without difficulty, the dog had to be very firmly kept in or he would force an exit and make his way back to the previous house. He did this on more than one occasion. If a cat is to be involved in a removal it is wise to keep it in for a few days before the move, transport it carefully in a basket with a lid, or a canvas bag with a zip fastener. Do not let it out until the removal men have left and all the doors are closed. Let the cat settle in the new house for a few days until it has become familiar with the lay-out and only let it out into the garden under supervision at first. Baskets like these are particularly useful if you ever want to take your pet to the vet, or to a show or even away on holiday.

Even more useful is a lead, if you can train your cat to become accustomed to it at an early age. Some breeds, particularly Siamese and Burmese, take quite naturally to it. Training to a collar should be the first thing, at about three months old. No grown cat will accept a collar without a struggle if it has not been trained as a kitten. It is also important to get the right kind of collar. Pet shops and animal welfare societies sell suitable elastic collars. Should your cat get caught when it is in a tree it will be able to slip out of a collar which will expand enough to go over its head.

The collar should be put on for only a few minutes each day at first. The kitten will almost certainly resist when the lead is put on but perseverance will give him the idea to walk a few steps. My cats always had the fixed impression that the lead prevented them from walking and would collapse on the floor in a heap refusing to move until they forgot and dashed off after a plaything. This is a handsome Blue Point Siamese out for a walk and obviously longing to be let free.

Whether your pet is one of the aristocrats, the best in show and prize-winner of all the awards, or just a lowly cat tattered and war torn, it has a just claim to your care and attention. There is not much doubt that most cats are well-loved but there are some that, because their owners lack the time or the knowledge, do appear to be rather neglected.

There are a number of animal welfare societies which are concerned that cats should receive proper attention and many of them run animal clinics if cost has to be considered when a cat is ill. The RSPCA has inspectors in Britain who will investigate cases of cruelty and neglect. The People's Dispensary for Sick Animals runs mobile dispensaries in Britain, on the Continent, in Egypt and South Africa. The Blue Cross Dumb Friends League is another organization devoted to this work. The Cats Protection League is concerned with abandoned cats.

Most countries are concerned that animals should not be ill-treated but in the West there are strict laws to protect animals from cruel practices. Dispatching animals from one place to another can cause distress unless proper care is paid to the method of packaging and worldwide legislation is urgently required on this matter. In Britain there is a Protection of Animals Act which makes it a punishable offence to cruelly ill-treat an animal and to cause it unnecessary suffering, this includes all animals not only cats. The Pet Animals Act, 1960, made it an offence to abandon an animal. Irresponsible people sometimes leave cats and kittens uncared for at holiday times, and unwanted kittens are sometimes taken from home and left to die. These are both offences under the Act. You do not require a licence to keep a cat, nor to breed cats. If a motorist accidentally kills a cat he does not have to report the accident but if the cat is injured in a road accident the motorist is liable to

prosecution if he does not do something to relieve its suffering.

You are not being kind to your cat if you spoil it by overfeeding. The cat will eat the food you give it, so you must control the quantity for the cat will not, and will still go out and hunt its own food. This is its natural behaviour pattern. An overfed cat will put on weight and become sluggish. It will be lazy, and will be unable to climb trees and will become very miserable. When kittens are born they weigh about four ounces. By six months they are about ninety per cent of their adult weight. When they are about a year old they gain their full adult weight which is, for a female between six and eight pounds. A tom should weigh a little more. The owner of this Long-haired Blue and White cat [*above right*] has kept him to a balanced diet so that he is in excellent condition and his body is correctly proportioned. Judges look for this at the show.

Acquiring a cat is like getting married. You take it for better or for worse. Fortunately the good times outnumber the bad but there are times when the cat is absolutely dependent on you, and that is when it is sick. On the whole, barring accidents, cats are usually extremely healthy. When they do get sick they go downhill fast and then specialist help is needed.

There are only two major illnesses which are likely to affect the cat. Of these, the most serious is Feline Infectious Enteritis. Once this is contracted it is almost certain to prove fatal but it can be avoided as inoculation is available and will give certain protection. When this illness has been present in a house no new kitten should be introduced until at least six months afterwards, and certainly not before it has been inoculated. The other serious illness is cat flu or distemper. This can cause death but if a veterinary surgeon is called in early he can treat it with antibiotics.

If you wish to preserve your furniture and your carpet it would be wise to provide your cat with a scratching post. Table legs or upholstery make an excellent alternative in your cat's eyes but you may not be prepared to make the sacrifices. A place to claw and stretch is essential as your cat will take every care of its only weapon. The claws are very important and must be kept clean and sharp. This the cat will do by scratching, pulling off the outer shell as it becomes worn. Scratching in this way also exercises the muscles and tendons. If your kitten insists on using the furniture you must train it to use the post you have provided by firmly saying 'No' and placing its paws gently on a log or solid board upholstered with carpet. If an ordinary log is used it must be replaced as soon as it becomes smooth and shiny. It is extremely difficult to resist a tiny kitten, especially one as adorable as this Long-haired White. Too often people take on a kitten without realizing that it will require attention: grooming, feeding, training and that sometimes it will get into mischief and often misbehave. The way a kitten develops depends very much on the owner and it will learn good habits with time and patience on the part of the owner. Children are often guilty of enthusing about a kitten and getting bored with it as it grows. It is important to remind children when they beg for a kitten that the responsibility will go on for many years and it must not be undertaken lightly. The law takes care of this as much as possible by making it an offence to sell an animal to a child under the age of twelve, but the rest is up to the parents.

Like all small creatures, the kitten needs plenty of fresh air and exercise if it is to grow into a healthy cat. Where there is a garden nearby there is no problem for the cat will know when it wants to go out and when it would like to rest and nothing you can say or do will make it change its mind. Generally when the cat is outside it will not need supervision for it is unlikely to stray far away and will usually appear when it is called. I say 'appear' for if, when you call, it is not ready to leave its game in the garden it will make off again. The cat is notoriously disobedient and self-willed. You cannot make a cat do anything that is not to its own advantage. Nor should you ever deprive a cat of its freedom to come and go at will, for in almost every instance he will return unless the circumstances are exceptional. A friend reported finding his cat after ten days absence. It had taken up residence at a local garage. Upon investigation I discovered the cat did not actually belong to my friend but was a neighbour's pet. The neighbour had gone away for a long holiday leaving my friend to care for the animal. Obviously the cat was wanting more company than my friend was able to offer. Cats have been known to cover great distances in search of lost owners. If you do leave your cat to be looked after by a neighbour it is advisable to keep it shut in the house with a litter tray to prevent it from straying.

The cat owner does not have to take his pet for a walk as he would a dog. The cat will decide for itself when it will take its exercise. The independent spirit of the cat is one of its charms, another is its extreme cleanliness. At a very early age the kitten learns from its mother how to use a litter tray. This is instinctive training for in the wild state all cats, including lions and tigers, learn to conceal evidence of their presence.

A young kitten must be provided with a sanitary tray, which can be an old baking tin, but with the sides low enough for the kitten to get into comfortably. A thick layer of soil, ashes, peat or proprietary brand of litter should be put in the tray and should be changed frequently as no cat will use a smelly tray. As the cat grows it must have complete freedom to go into the garden as it wishes. The simplest way to achieve this is to have a cat door fitted to one of the outside doors of the house. Sir Isaac Newton is said to have had two cat doors cut for his pets; there was a small door for the kitten, and a larger one for its mother. Cats quickly learn how to use a flap and even enjoy it.

It is not an unusual sight in the garden to see a cat stalking in the long grass. A gentle breeze catches the surface like a ripple on a stream, a sudden leap and another insect has been taken unawares. Cats love hunting the creepy crawlies that live in the undergrowth. They also like eating the grass itself. It is a natural medicine and all cats should have access to some. If you live in a town and have no garden, grass should be provided in a pot or box. Cocksfoot grass is the favourite and if you sow some every week or ten days your cat will be delighted.

Cat fur ball is most common in Long-haired cats although it can occur in all cats, particularly when the cat is moulting. It is most likely to develop when there are large quantities of hair available to swallow, too much for the cat to cope with through the normal processes. The cat does, of course, swallow a large amount of hair when it is doing its routine grooming but it naturally ejects this. Occasionally it does get rather too much for the cat, the stomach becomes distended and it becomes a job for the vet. He will deal with this medically or in very severe cases, with the aid of surgery. Frequent grooming to remove all loose hair will minimize the risk. Small doses of liquid paraffin in the cat's milk perhaps twice a week, will keep the contents of the intestine moving freely and prevent the fur from collecting and causing discomfort.

# Siamese and Oriental Cats

Siamese are probably the most popular of all pedigree breeds at the present time; they are fashionable in the same way as poodles were a fashionable breed of dog in the 1960's. I feel very unhappy when an animal becomes fashionable because it tends to become overbred and either the features are exaggerated or weaknesses creep in. If you want a Siamese kitten you would be well advised to go to a recognized breeder to be sure of getting a good strain. There are Siamese Cat Clubs both in Britain and the United States which will be very happy to give advice about where to obtain a kitten.
It is well worth while making up your mind whether you want a kitten for showing or just for a pet before you buy it, since you would be wise, obviously enough, to choose a good example if you are wanting a particular breed and have hopes of showing it. A pet should be neutered or altered or you may find yourself perpetrating a fault.
Siamese cats love company and will readily strike up a friendship with other animals in the household providing they are introduced properly. No sensible person would leave two animals alone together until they are sure both animals have accepted each other, which may take quite a few days. The animal that is in residence first will be anxious to protect its

territory and the newcomer will be feeling strange and very tense, very much on the defensive. Care and common sense on these occasions can prevent much distress. A quick clean up after dinner and then these two [*above*] will settle down for a nap . . . this is a Chocolate Point Siamese and an Irish Wolfhound. The cat's points should be considerably lighter than those of a Seal Point and be the colour of milk chocolate. The coat should be pale cream with no shading.
In 1962 three breeders in Britain crossed some Siamese cats with White Short-haired cats. The white kittens born as a result had the Foreign body type with a coat of pure white and were called Foreign Whites [*left*]. This cat has been bred through successive generations and no doubt in time will be awarded a class number at the shows. A cat similar in Type but descended from the Lilac Point Siamese is the Foreign Lilac, known in the United States as the Lavender. It has a coat of faded lavender with no shading on the points and mask. The eyes, like those of the Foreign White, are Oriental in shape and are a vivid apple green. Breeders mating Lilac to Lilac are able to breed true to type and colour and it should not be long before these delicately coloured cats also receive recognition at the show.

pointed cats do vary quite distinctly and consistently and breeders say that Blue Points have gentler natures than the Seal Point and that the Tabby Point [*below right*] is the most accommodating of all the Siamese. Clearly demonstrating the Siamese type of head, eyes and ears, is a Blue Pointed Siamese [*left and below*] and a Seal Point [*right*].

Like several other breeds there are stories of the Siamese origins which will not stand up to investigation. One popular belief is that the breed was first brought out from the Buddhist temples, but this honour has also been accorded to the Birman cat. The story is pure myth in both cases for there are no sacred cats in the Buddhist temples. It has also been said the first pair were a present from the King of Spain to the British Consul-General in Bangkok but the particulars of this story are confused. One account states that the pair arrived in England in 1886 and another that it was in 1884. There is more evidence of their existence at a later date, in 1892 the first standard of points for Siamese was published in 'Our Cats', this was in the

The head of the Siamese is long, well proportioned, and tapers to the nose in straight lines. Eyes are slanting, set wide apart, of a deep, sapphire blue and with no suggestion of a squint. In the past Siamese have frequently had a squint in the eyes but careful selection has practically erased this fault. Its ears must look larger than those of any other domestic cat, they should be long and wide at the base. The Siamese carries its ears well-pricked and they should be rather pointed at the tip. The type is the same for all Siamese cats, the difference in the varieties is in the colour of the points. The characters of the differently

early days of the Cat Fancy in Britain. There are conflicting stories about the first Siamese cats to appear in America, also. Many different people are alleged to be the first Siamese owners.

It is not difficult to imagine these cats as 'royal' cats with their long, lightly built bodies, thin, straight legs and dainty feet. Old illustrations of the Siamese show how the cat has changed in appearance with the aid of careful breeding. The early cats had rounder heads and the coat was darker. All the early Siamese had a kink in the tail, today a kink tail is considered a fault. There is a legend which tells how the Siamese came by its kinked tail. A Royal Princess left her precious rings to the care of her cat while she bathed in the river. She placed them on its tail but unfortunately the cat forgot they were there and they fell off and were lost. On the next occasion the Princess bent the end of the tail over as a precaution against further loss, and so the kink stayed in the tail.

This Tabby Point Siamese is a most attractive cat. It has all the traditional qualities of the Siamese but in addition it

has this quite outstanding coloration. The original Siamese Tabby Points were the results of a mis-alliance between a Seal Point Siamese female and a male of Tabby origin. Since the gene for Tabby marking is dominant, the kittens born carried the pattern on the mask and points. The pale beauty of the coat

highlighted by the pencilled tabby markings was enchanting and the variety was developed further. Tabby-Point owners say their cats are more gentle than most other Siamese varieties. In the United States of America the Tabby Point is known as the Lynx Point Siamese.

It is the dream of every breeder to produce a cat which captures the attention of everyone at the show. Siamese breeders are no exception and they have developed cats in varying colour combinations to enhance the breed. Already recognized are the Red Point, Lilac or Frost Point and more recently the Tabby Point. These are in addition to the original Seal, Chocolate and Blue Points. Now permutations of all these colours are appearing in the masks and points, each with the addition of cream in the basic colours. These are known as Tortie Points, they have only recently received official recognition. There must be no Tabby markings, the colours must be patched or mingled as in Tortoiseshell cats. There is a breed number now for 'Any Other Colour Siamese'; this is to cover any future Siamese bred with points of a colour not yet recognized.

The senior member of the Siamese breed is the Seal Point and many owners remain loyal to this elegant cat with mask, ears, legs, feet and tail all a rich brown. A regal animal showing class from the tip of its aristocratic nose to the end of its tail is 'Black Bart' [left], the finest Seal Point Siamese in the United States today.

The Lilac Point Siamese has a delicate appearance with its fine bones and pastel colouring but it is, in fact, as hardy as the other Siamese. There is sometimes confusion when the kittens begin to develop their darker-coloured points as to which variety they are going to be, and the safest way to be certain is to check the pads on the feet. A Chocolate Point has pads of pale brown, those of a Blue Point are grey but those of a Lilac are frosty grey, or of a pinkish tone.

A female cat was taken from Burma to the United States in 1930 and was mated with a Siamese male. The males from the resulting litter were mated back to the mother and sired dark, brown cats of foreign type which became known as Brown Burmese. In order to establish a breed they had to breed true for several generations so it was not until 1936 that these cats received official recognition in America. They did not arrive in Britain until the late 1940's and did not receive official status until 1952. You can see from this history that a great deal of patience is required if you aspire to great things in cat breeding. There can be many disappointments but there is also a great deal of satisfaction, especially when the cat finally reaches dizzy heights as the Burmese has done.

They are less vocal than the Siamese, and also less nervous and less highly strung. In fact, most Burmese are extremely placid and calm; one of their special qualities is their gentleness. This does not mean they lack character for they have the reputation of being some of the most lively and energetic of pets. They are particularly intelligent and have been known to persevere for hours to open doors and windows, often with amazing success. They are singularly friendly cats; even the kittens seem anxious to make friends with you right away, and are not in the least shy and retiring.

The body of the Burmese is foreign in type but not so long as that of its Siamese ancestors. It should be medium in size, elegant and svelte, with the neck long and slender. The legs should be in proportion to the body, slim and long, and the hind legs should be slightly longer than the front legs. The face of the Burmese should be wedge-shaped, but the features are somewhat softer looking than the Siamese being shorter and blunter and a little wider at the jaw hinge. The top of the head is slightly rounded; the ears should be large at the base, set well apart and rounded at the tip. From a front view the outer line of the ears should continue the wedge shape of the face.

When the kittens are born they are coffee coloured, coffee with cream in fact. As

they grow older they gradually become
darker until, when they are about two
years old they develop the really dark,
chocolate brown colour, although the
chest and underparts still tend to be
paler. Their Siamese ancestry can be seen
in the kittens and sometimes never quite
disappears.

The kink in the tail is sometimes still
found in the Burmese, at one time it was
a characteristic of the breed but now it is
considered undesirable.

Their eyes have a most unusual
characteristic. The standard requires that
they be shades of yellow or gold but the
tendency is for the majority to have eyes
of chartreuse yellow which is a greenish
yellow. When the eyes are being judged
for colour they are apt to be affected by
the colour and light of the place where
the cats are, as they have such a low
colour density. It is preferable to look at
them in moderately strong, diffuse
daylight, and the Burmese Cat Club
supplies the judges with a piece of
chartreuse yellow silk ribbon against
which to compare the eyes.

One of the most attractive features of the
Burmese cat is its close lying, glossy coat.
A cat that is in good condition really has
a beautiful sheen. When a litter of kittens
was produced in 1955, there was among
them a kitten with a blue-grey coat.
Today that kitten is a forebear of the Blue
Burmese, which is now a well established
variety in Britain, Europe and the United
States. The colour of the adult cat is
bluish grey, a warm colour with the high
gloss giving it a silver effect. In every
other way it is like the Brown Burmese.
This Blue Burmese [right] is about to
settle down for a good wash and Brown
Burmese kittens are playing in the
background.

A range of new colours in the Burmese
cat is now beginning to appear, there will
soon be quite a collection from which to
choose. There is Cream, Red, Blue Cream
and Tortoiseshell. Cream and Blue Cream
have very recently been granted breed
numbers but Red and Tortoiseshell must
still be entered in the 'Any Other Variety'
section at a show.

The cat world is full of conflicting stories about the origins of certain cats, and the Abyssinian is the centre of one of these controversies. Some breeders maintain this cat is a descendant of the ancient, sacred cats of Egypt while some others believe it came to Britain from Abyssinia at the end of the nineteenth century. There are no cats in Abyssinia today that fit the description so the origins must remain a mystery. However, of all the domestic cats seen in the world today, the Abyssinian most resembles the domestic cats which were worshipped in Ancient Egypt, according to the descriptions and illustrations in old wall paintings in museums and elsewhere. The Abyssinian is rabbit-coloured and is sometimes called 'bunny-cat'. The coat is described as being ticked, this means that each black hair is banded with brown. White hairs anywhere but on the chin are not appreciated by the judges. The cat is decidedly foreign in type; the tail is exceptionally long, the golden, greeny eyes have the typical Oriental slant and almond shape, the head is long and pointed, and the ears are large and broad and are frequently tipped with hairs like those of a lynx. Abyssinians are hardy cats which like plenty of freedom. They are extremely active and even when adult are very playful; many of them love to retrieve objects just like a dog. Attractive and very intelligent, these cats demand plenty of affection and will give you much in return, as well as amusing companionship. They have delightful temperaments and are known for their strength and courage. In contrast to the Siamese, they have soft voices and hardly ever use them. Normally they do not have large families and if you wish to obtain a cat of this breed you may have to be patient and wait a while before you can have a kitten.

The Red Abyssinian [*left*] is one of the cats to have recently received a class number and a standard of points. The black ticking is absent on the coat and the colour is a solid copper red. When the Abyssinians were first recognized kittens of this colour appeared from time to time and breeders were barred from showing an otherwise splendid specimen because the copper red colour did not fit the breed. Eventually they were recognized as a separate variety and today the Red Abyssinian is a breed in its own right. In the United States this cat, with its little pink pads, is known as the 'Sorrel'

There is no proof that the Russian Blue [*top left*] was ever bred in Russia, although there are some who say the cat was known a century ago as the Archangel Cat.

This cat is easily distinguishable from the British Blue because it is of a foreign type. The body is long and graceful, the head with flat skull has the typical foreign wedge-shaped nose, the ears are large and pointed, and are very fine and transparent. The Russian Blue has prominent whisker pads. Its special feature is the beautiful thick coat of silvery blue, like seal-skin, which when brushed back clearly shows the undercoat. In contrast with the blue of the coat the eyes are of vivid green. They should be almond shaped, not set too closely together.

One of the rarest recognized breeds all over the world is the Havanna cat [*left*]. Given a breed number in 1958 it was also given the name Chestnut Brown Foreign to avoid wild stories being invented about its origin. This cat occurred first because of a mismating between a Black Long-haired female and a Seal Point Siamese. One of the black female kittens born as a result was again mated with a Siamese and in the litter was an all-brown male. This was a forerunner of a new breed. The cats are a warm mahogany brown all over in colour, and are of foreign type with a low wedge-shaped head set on a graceful

neck. The eyes are chartreuse green, oval in shape and set almost straight, and the Americans describe this cat as having a pixie look.

The short, glossy coat may have no shadow points, as may occasionally be seen in the Burmese. The kittens sometimes show tabby 'ghost' markings but these soon disappear.

In the United States in 1954 there appeared by chance a cat with a long flowing coat in a litter of pure bred Siamese. This was not the cat from which the Colourpoint developed, since it retained its Siamese type and it did not have the ruff and frill of the Long-haired cats. The Balinese, as it was called, is tall and of aristocratic appearance. The body is of foreign type, long and svelte, and it has dainty legs, neck and tail, with paws that are small and oval. The head is wedge-shaped like that of the Siamese, and the ears large, pricked and wide. The face has an intelligent expression and the eyes are large and round. It is a Siamese cat with a long silky coat, and in a perfect specimen the coat is at least two inches in length. The Colourpoint on the other hand is a Long-haired cat with Siamese colouring, so that it has the Persian build and shape. The Governing Council of the Cat Fancy does not yet recognize the Balinese as a separate breed.

# White Cats

In 1871 an artist and cat lover by the name of Harrison Weir organized a cat show at the Crystal Palce. He wanted the public to see the beauty of the cat. There were cats of all kinds at the show and it was not very long after this that the 'Cat Fancy' was introduced. Mr Weir's own particular passion was for white cats, particularly Long-haired white cats. He described the show in this way:

'There they lay in their different pens, reclining on crimson cushions, making no sound save now and then a homely purring, as from time to time they lapped the nice new milk provided for them. Yes, there they were, big cats, very big cats, middling sized cats, and small cats of all colours and markings, and beautiful White Persian cats . . .'

Today there are many more cats than ever appeared then but still the white Persians win the admiration at the show.

The standard for White Long-hairs requires that they should have a round, broad head with small ears set wide apart. The body should be cobby and compact, there should be no hint of coarseness, and the legs should be thick and sturdy. The coat should be pure white without a mark or shade of any kind, and should be long and flowing on the body. The immense ruff should continue in a deep frill between the front legs, the tail should be short and full. Long-haired cats are generally known as Persians, they first appeared in Europe towards the end of the sixteenth century. White Persians can have blue, green, orange or yellow eyes and some have odd eyes. If you want your cat for show purposes, however, there are class numbers only for Blue, Orange or the Odd-eyed Whites. White cats with eyes of green or yellow must be shown in the class for household pets.

these itself and it may cause hairballs to form in the stomach. At the very least the cat will be uncomfortable and it can lead to more severe complications.

Eye colour is important when cats are being examined for quality. This is particularly so in the case of White cats whose eyes dictate which class number they shall be exhibited in. There are three distinct varieties of White Long-hair, one which has blue eyes, one which has eyes that are deep orange in colour, and a third that is the result of cross mating the first two which has produced a cat with one orange eye and one blue, the Odd-eyed White.

The Blue-eyed White is the oldest breed of the three. It is not really known from whence they originate. The first long-haired cats were called 'Angoras' and it was alleged they came from Ankara, later they came to be known as Persians and were said to come from Persia. There are references to white cats with long hair in the Middle East in the seventeenth century and definite evidence that they were in France at least two hundred years ago.

Generally speaking, Blue-eyed Whites are not as good in type as those which have orange eyes and unfortunately they have the added disadvantage that a great many of them are incurably deaf. It is believed that this may be due to partial albinism, a feature of albinism is deafness, and the fact that their eyes glint red in certain lights would seem to support this theory. Some of the owners of the Odd-eyed Whites claim their cats have imperfect hearing, but they are never stone deaf. In an effort to eliminate the gene for deafness, and in order to improve the coat the Blue-eyed White was mated with a cat of another colour with orange eyes and in all probability that is how the Orange-eyed White first appeared as a distinct breed.

White Long-hairs are extremely glamorous cats. They are perfectly aware of their beauty and very proud of their appearance so they will spend a great deal of time grooming and keeping themselves clean. The owner must give some aid in this direction by combing through the long hairs twice every day.

This is necessary not only in order to keep the cat's appearance in tip-top condition, but if this is neglected your pet's health will suffer. Cats which are given the freedom to roam in the garden often get twigs and prickles caught in the long hair. The hair will matt if these are not removed, the cat will try to remove

Dignity and pride they may have, but they will quite often forget both and behave like kittens [*right*] until they recollect their age! They also like nothing better than to stretch and roll as this one is about to do. His expression is an open invitation for play. Once the 'chase' begins it is the cat that wins; so controlled are its movements and so alert is it to every move that you can make, that he will not be caught until he is ready for surrender, which will be long after you have tired of the game!

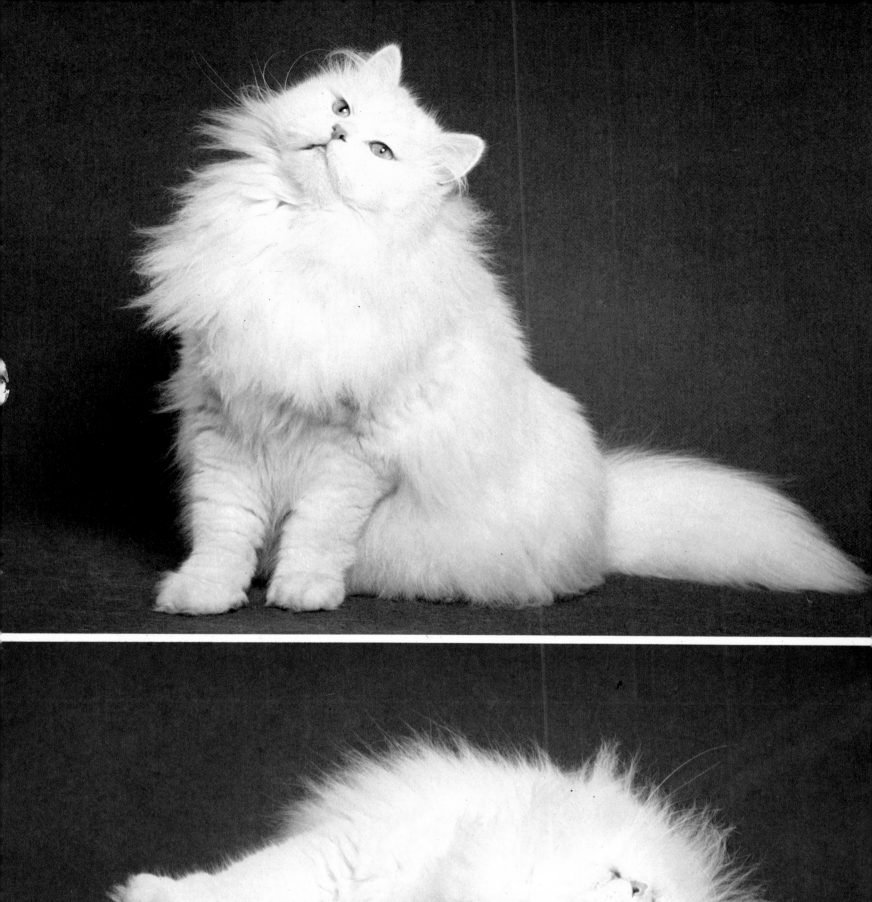

The Odd-eyed White cat has been a recognized breed for a long time in the United States of America, in Britain its inclusion as a variety with a class number of its own is recent. White kittens are often born with a few black hairs on their heads, but these soon disappear as the kitten grows older. There must be no black hairs when the kittens are shown. The coat must be a pure, clear white, as there are objections to a cream or bluish tinge in the coat. The colour of the eyes must be one deep blue and one orange eye, pale eye colour is considered a fault. They should appear as jewels against the flawless, white background, as they do in this picture [above].

Many people interested in showing hesitate to keep a white cat because of the difficulty in maintaining the purity of colour. If the coat is to retain its attraction a lot of attention must be paid to grooming. Frequent use of powder followed by careful brushing will do much to remove dirt and grease from the coat. At times the coat will assume a yellowish tinge caused by grease from the skin combined with dirt from the air. When this happens a cat may be bathed, but as this is not his favourite way to spend an afternoon this should not be done too frequently. Warm bran rubbed into the coat with the finger tips and brushed out thoroughly is a highly desirable

alternative. Cats who show traces of powder in the coat may be disqualified from showing so it is important to complete this part of its preparation well in advance, a few days or so, in order to clear the fur completely.

Although the Chinchilla has such an aristocratic appearance, it is not in the least haughty. In fact, this cat is very affectionate and easy to please, and is a great favourite as much for this reason as for its beauty. It is thought that the Chinchilla may have been bred from Silver Tabby crossed with Tortoiseshell and White, the Long-haired varieties. There is some evidence to support this idea because as can be seen the kittens have faint tabby markings for the first few weeks [right]. When these are only on the back and tail they very quickly disappear, but any barring on the legs, however, is more stubborn and sometimes never fades completely which could prevent an adult cat from becoming a prize winner.

Chinchillas are very hardy cats, despite their ethereal appearance. They are good travellers and have been exported from Great Britain to many parts of the world. They do not seem unduly disturbed by a journey and it is the ease with which they settle down that makes them so suitable for filming.

Foolish is the person who thinks fences will keep a cat at home. If it is important to keep your cat in it must be kept in a run with a roof. All cats are expert climbers and few barriers are insurmountable. It is difficult to keep kittens on ground level, they simply adore the struggle to reach a great height and then the challenge to get down again. Even inside the house, kittens prefer walking on tops of furniture rather than on the ground. It is possibly part of their instinctive caution that makes them like to be high up. However, haring through the grass well away from the danger of human feet is another thing altogether [*below left*].

Cats love sunbathing too [*below right*] and always manage to find an ideal place such as this warm, smooth stone where they can bask in the bright sunlight and also be noticed and admired by as many people as possible, as cats love admiration. And of course their chosen spot will nearly always be high up. However a cat will sometimes deliberately lie right in the middle of a path or terrace or drive so as to be so conspicuous as to be safe and inevitably attract the maximum amount of attention.

This magnificent creature resting on a pylon on the bridge at Sydney Harbour doesn't need a sign-post to show him the way, he has reached the top already. That feathery brush is obviously his pride and his pose displays it to full advantage. The tail is indicative of many moods, it will convey much to those who take the trouble to learn the gesture language of cats. For example, a swishing tail is a sign that a cat is upset and if this warning is not heeded it is likely to get really angry. A cat deep in thought will sit bolt upright, just twitching the end of its tail. When a cat walks away from you with its tail carried high above its back it is an expression of independence and complete indifference. When the tip is just turned over however, then the cat is feeling pretty pleased with itself. There are many more twitches and positions, in fact a whole 'tail language' which varies slightly with every cat and which you will find you know intimately after living with your own pet for some time.

The Foreign White [*right*] is a cat not yet recognized as a breed by the Governing Council of the Cat Fancy although there is a Foreign White Cat Society which is working towards this end. At the moment members wishing to show their cats must exhibit them as 'Any Other Variety'. This cat exactly resembles the Siamese in body shape, it has the typical foreign body, long and svelte, the wedge-shaped head bearing the large, pricked, wide-based ears, the long, whip-like tail. The coat is pure white with no shading whatsoever on the points and mask. The Foreign White has the almond-shaped, slanting eyes of the Orientals, they are a deep, vivid blue. Although white cats with blue eyes are invariably deaf the genetic make-up of this cat is different so that it has excellent hearing and no other inherited defects. This is a cat worth watching in the future.

# Dedication
# to Cats

All females, unless they have been spayed, will become mothers, this is as inevitable as night will follow day. If you are going to keep brood queens in the house only two or three should be kept, four at the most. If more than four are kept special accommodation should be provided or there will be great problems when the kittens begin to arrive.

An outdoor cattery is preferable. A shed built of weather board, and lined with plywood to keep out draughts, is ideal. It must have plenty of ventilation. The furniture for this cattery need not be elaborate. There should be sleeping boxes and litter trays for use at night. A shelf running right round the house at a height of about two feet from the floor should be provided, cats need to have somewhere to leap to and from. Outside there should be a run built like a large cage. In it, there should be grass, a tree trunk, both to climb and to use for a scratching post, and some ledge or platform where the cats can laze or bask in the sun, preferably two or three of these high shelves.

No cat likes to be confined, or to be without company and this should only happen when 'needs must'. Calling queens cannot be put together and must prowl out their season alone like this wistful Tabby Point Siamese [below]. The lovely Colourpoints [left] are in good company and are in excellent conditions in a boarding cattery, which is often the solution to holiday problems. If you are not able to take your cat away with you then a good boarding cattery where it can be left is the answer. You must take care when choosing one, it is wise to inspect it before making a booking. Ideally the houses and runs should be as described above, and should be quite separate to avoid the risk of infection. On no account must you put food down at home and leave the cat to look after itself. The cat will not know how to ration its meals and will either eat it all up at once, or the left-over food will become stale and probably fly-blown.

If you take a cat abroad you must remember that a cat cannot re-enter Britain without going straight into quarantine for six months. This is enforced, with no exceptions, for all cats and dogs to prevent the re-introduction of rabies into the country. There are government approved catteries where the cat is detained and isolated for six calendar months from the date of landing. The cost of boarding is the responsibility of the owner. Visiting is allowed during this period and owners are advised to visit as frequently as possible, but of course the necessity of six months in quarantine prevents the majority of people from taking their pets abroad. It is a miserable time for the animals and for their owners too.

The cat is notoriously promiscuous [*left*]. Left to its own devices it begins its breeding season soon after Christmas and continues until some time in September. It may thus have a litter of kittens in March, another in June and a third in the autumn. Unlike dogs, cats do not come into season twice a year and there is no time cycle. If the female is not mated it will come into season again almost at once and the cycles will continue until the cat is mated.

A pedigree queen, kept in the controlled conditions of a cattery, confined and warm, is usually only allowed two litters each year, one in spring and one in the early autumn. Although she will have reached sexual maturity at between five and six months old, she should be restrained from mating until she is at least ten months old because she will not have the physical maturity. In an underdeveloped queen the result could be serious.

You will know when your female is in season for she will begin to call. This is an unmistakable noise, a wild cry which can be heard over great distances. An indication that she is about to begin calling is extreme restlessness. She is likely to roll over and over, howling or rushing about making mewing noises. Until you complete your arrangements to send the queen away to stud, she must be kept away from all males.

The calling of a cat in oestrus will attract males from a wide area. It has been said the call of a Siamese queen can be heard for six miles over open country. On the other hand, some Persian and most non-pedigree cats make very little noise and sometimes none at all, so it is extremely difficult to know exactly when your cat is in season. It is not easy to keep a female away from the males which take up the challenge of a call, and you as well as your cat, will be serenaded with their eerie caterwauling. If your pedigree cat is not to mismanage her own affairs she must be kept very confined at this time.

Your queen will probably find her journey to the stud unusual and disturbing, and will also feel nervous and strange when she arrives so she must be allowed time to recover before being introduced to the tom. Even though this is an arranged match she will want to be given a chance to get acquainted. If the two cats are put into adjoining pens they will make friends through the wire and after a while they will begin to croon to each other, which is a sign that they are ready to be released.

The period of gestation in cats is variable, it can be anything between 57 and 69 days. It is difficult for at least four weeks after mating to know whether it was successful. When you first get your brood queen home after she has been to stud it is advisable to keep her confined for three weeks in case she needs to be returned for another service. If she is not confined she may make her own arrangements and present you with an unexpected litter.

The Chocolate Point Siamese kittens [*top left*] are just four days old. All they want to do at this stage in their lives is, like babies, to feed and sleep. Their mother will look after their needs until they are about eight weeks old, she will provide their food, wash them and teach them to be clean. From about two months old they must be weaned away from the mother and taught to be independent. The breeders will have begun to introduce the kittens to cow's milk sometime after they are four weeks old by dipping their noses in a saucer for a moment. By the time they can lap up milk unaided, and

they can take up to four weeks to learn this, they will be quite familiar with the flavour. No kitten should leave its mother before it is weaned completely. It should be fed little and often for the tiny stomach is only about the size of a walnut. Milk and meat should never be given together, nor should it be given straight from the refrigerator, all food should be given at room temperature. There are many well established rules to follow and a good breeder will give you a diet sheet and feeding instructions for your kitten.

The picture on the bottom of the previous page could be an ancestral portrait of the Colourpoint, for breeding of this variety first began by mating a Siamese with a Long-haired cat. Breeders of some new cat, having perfected the variety and having produced three successive generations, will want other people to see the result. This is where the Cat Show plays its part, and fanciers welcome the opportunity to display the result of their patience and scientific knowledge. It is from the exhibition that breeders get their publicity, and when their cats do well on the show bench they become popular, and it is popular demand that helps a new type of cat to become established.

The novice breeder should not make the mistake of keeping a tom as this is definitely a matter for the specialist. In order to keep a vigorous tom in the peak of condition, and to keep him from becoming bad tempered and noisy, perhaps even savage, his sexual needs must be satisfied. Two or three females of your own would be insufficient and to advertise his services elsewhere introduces the risk of infection from visiting queens. A stud tom is positively not a pet cat, he requires special accommodation away from the house.

For one thing, the house would soon smell of cat, for a tom will spray. This is not an indication of a dirty cat as is sometimes mistakenly believed, but rather the mating signal of the male. Stud toms can also be very noisy, and this can make you very unpopular with neighbours, especially at night. They are just as appealing as females when young, however, as is this six months-old Short-haired Black [*above left*], so it must be remembered that they will grow up less attractive.

If you are open minded about the kind of cat you would like to have, but you would like to own a pedigree cat, the wisest plan is to visit a cat show where all varieties of cats may be seen. This could, of course, complicate your decision for the most beautiful cats are on display and you could find making a choice very difficult. Almost certainly one variety will appeal to you more than

the others in the end. Shows are held in many parts of the country in the autumn and winter, they are usually advertised in the local paper. At the show you will meet the people exhibiting the kind of cat which appeals to you and they will advise you about obtaining a kitten. Once you have selected your breed it would be both sensible and interesting to join a cat club. They will give advice on many aspects of cat ownership.

However, it often happens that offers of kittens and pleas to take one of a charming but inevitably unwanted litter off the hands of cat owners looking for homes are showered upon you once it is known that you want a cat. Or you might see and fall for someone else's cat, like this beautiful Blue Burmese [*left*], and then, if there are no kittens planned, it would be a good idea to go to a show or write to the club to find out where a well-bred kitten is to be found.

All over the world there are dedicated cat breeders trying to produce the perfect cat. Like gardeners tending their precious blooms, they breed for colour, type, texture of coat, colour of eye. It is at the cat shows that the result of all this patience and loving care is put to the test.

The first official cat show took place at the Crystal Palace in London, in 1871. The organizer and judge at this event was Mr Harrison Weir. Six years later a group of cat lovers decided to form the National Cat Club which in 1910 combined with a rival body to form the Governing Council of the Cat Fancy. England was the only place in the world to have an organization of this kind. The American Cat Fanciers Inc. is now the largest body for registering cats and, after the Second World War, the European Cat Fancy was formed but the standards of points in both continents are based on the British equivalent.

In Britain a cat may not be exhibited at the show until it has been registered with the Governing Council of the Cat Fancy. There are many rules for showing but a copy of those issued by the Cat Fancy are sent out with the entry forms. These should be studied carefully as a simple error could cause disqualification.

The details on the entry form must correspond with those on the cat's registration form. Kittens are usually registered by the breeder soon after they are born. Since cats can only be shown in the name of the owner it is important to check that notice of transfer of ownership has been given to the registrar of the governing body on completion of sale.

Breeders of pedigree cats usually adopt a prefix by which the cattery can be identified so that when the cat is registered the prefix precedes its given name. It is a guarantee of quality, for the breeder is demonstrating confidence in his own cats. Left are three striking Red Point Siamese kittens aged six months.

Great care is taken at the show to prevent the spread of infection. Before the show begins all the cats are vetted in, which means that no exhibit is admitted to the show hall until it has been examined by the veterinary surgeon. If he suspects some illness, or if he finds fleas in the fur or mites in the ears he will probably decide the cat must be isolated or sent home. All cats are subjected to this examination including those entered as unregistered.

Each class has a judge and steward who give their services voluntarily. In Britain the judge goes to the pen where the cat is lifted on to a small table by the steward. Before any cat is handled both the judge and steward wash their hands in disinfectant. In North America and on the Continent, the cats are carried to the judge, and in America the owner may carry the cat to the judge; elsewhere it is the responsibility of the steward. In Britain the owner is not allowed to assist even if the cat is difficult to handle.

Cat shows in Britain are one day affairs, though on the Continent they sometimes last for two days. While some cats enjoy the exhibition and the fuss and attention they receive, there are others that behave quite out of character and become vicious. However the cat reacts, it is a certainty that at the end of the day it will be very tired. By the time it reaches home it may also be cold, for cat shows are usually held in the autumn and winter when the female cats are least likely to be in season. On reaching home the cat should receive special attention. It should have a tasty meal and a warm bed, and some breeders give a little brandy or whisky in warm milk. The cat should be wiped gently all over with a mild disinfectant, paying special attention to the paws, corner of the eyes, mouth and ears. It should not be allowed contact with other cats and kittens for at least a few days as a precaution against introducing infection.

# Index

# Acknowledgments

*The Publishers would like to thank the following organizations and individuals for their kind permission to reproduce the pictures in this book:*

Baldwin, Victor: 30, 53, 56 top, 78, 84, 85, 90
Barnaby's Picture Library: 49, 83 bottom
Bisserôt, Sdeuard: 19 bottom, 25, 32 bottom, 33, 42 bottom, 48, 54, 55, 58 top, 59, 66 top, 67 top, 70 below, 76 top, 83 top, 91 bottom, 99, 102 top
Grossaner J., ZEFA: 29
Holford, Michael, Ianthe Ruthven: 22
Kalt, Gerolf, Bavaria Verlag: 3, 4, 23 top
Kalt, Gerolf, ZEFA: 1, 23 bottom
Keystone: 66 bottom
Leidmann, Bavaria Verlag: 9
Lüthy, W., Bavaria Verlag: 14 top, 19 top, 61, 64, 82

Miller, Jane: 16 bottom, 31 right, 34, 43, 87, 92, 93, 94
Mohn, ZEFA: 45
Smith Peter, Animal Photography: 15, 37, 57, 63, 67 bottom, 100, 101 top
Spectrum: 18, 24, 25, 28 top, 31 left, 44 bottom, 60, 65, 71, 95
Thompson, Sally Anne, Animal Photography: 2, 3, 6, 7, 8 top, 11, 12, 13, 14 bottom, 16 top, 17, 20, 21, 24, 32 top, 35, 36, 38, 39, 40, 41, 42 top, 44 top, 46, 47, 50, 51, 52, 56 bottom, 58 bottom, 62, 68, 70 top, 72, 73, 74, 75, 76 bottom, 77 bottom, 79, 80, 81 88, 89, 91, 96, 97, 98, 99 bottom, 100 bottom, 102 bottom, 103
Wegler M, ZEFA: 28 bottom
Whitmore, Betty Griffin: 86